Belle's Ragged Army

Joan Burt

Grateful acknowledgement to the editors of the following
reviews where these poems first appeared:
The Santa Fe Literary Review, "My Mother's Hands," 2014;
The Bosque Review 6, "Burning Lady," 2016;
The Bosque Review 7, "The Nylon Couch of Our Family
Room," and "Auntie Mattie I: Kitchen Table," 2017.

ISBN 978-0-9985140-5-5
Printed in the United States of America

RED MOUNTAIN PRESS
Santa Fe, New Mexico
www.redmountainpress.us

For Steve

A Note from the Author

Nothing ever happens the way it happened.

In the house that I was born into there were wonderful picnics, with my dad and his polka-dot hat directing the campfire smoke. Thanks to warm Chinook winds these outings occurred every several weeks, by old trails, rivers, lakes and streams.

We experienced suicide, professional Ag papers, bird dogs, alcoholism, deep Nebraska roots, post-breakfast bridge and pitch games lasting into twilight, Alzheimer's disease, normalized mental illness, and, across the street, Shakespeare in the Park.

All of it was the crunchy nougat inside childhood dreams.

I write poems because of their curative power and because, for me so far, crafting them is the most effective activity for capturing and softening my feelings. It's like scooping out the bone marrow of my past with sticks and teaspoons, in soft hunks.

Joan Burt
Santa Fe, New Mexico
May 2018

SCARS

My body has pains in it and I put them there.
I wear the scars like a badge of honor.
Sparkling, circling gemstones
have lit the way
on this path
of silvery scars.

Memories, attach to places, then my body
marks itself with deep things
underneath,
with thoughts of embarrassment,
my daily dose of shame presented,
stashed among them,
all bunched under my skin.

Winding up tighter, electrons swirling
in my atom's pants

       positioning
       quickening
       springing
       ricocheting

       too much
       not enough
       not really right
       all right now.

BELLE AT HER KITCHEN SINK

Belle thinks of her relatives, whistles
while she works. Then leans down
 in front of her sink, whistles
an octave higher and a little more sweetly, singing
"I Love a Parade."

A pair of legs, Allen's, arrested, stumbles
down the middle of the street.
The stolen camper shell moves slowly
down the pavement,
a roach, carried on her nephew's bent-over back.

The rain slides down the windowpane
as Belle reaches out to touch her palm
to the open window and to smell
the air. Belle claims she has the most sensitive
nose, her pride, her animal burden.

There is a dimming southern exposure.
A handmade knife-holder is at eye-level.
Tucked behind the row of knives,
barely seen behind the standing knife handles,
as if *incarcerated*,

a small, beaming head-shot of my father.

Ballerina

He says he can do anything he wants once
inside this form. My Aunt Alyce sent me
a music box that plays his waltz music—
"Tales from the Vienna Woods."

There is a three-sided mirror in the purple-lined
lid of the box. The little dancer pops up
with a flourish.
I touch her. I feel the stiff nylon net of her tutu,
watch her spin around.

I like making her twirl. I wear her out, she comes off
her armature.

Before I learn what Strauss said
about the music,
about his secret freedom.

I Want to Get Off

Belle sits behind a shiny visitor's desk.
Above her, a grotesquely elongated,
model of Earth.

Wires around the globe suspend
sailing corporate containers:
> Hellmann's, Heinz, Birds Eye, Wishbone.

Our gal is tiny below the floating icons.
With red lipstick and cat's-eye glasses,
she welcomes the public
to the world of industrial condiments.

It is very Belle,
this effort to create a flimsy empire.

She has a complete lack of embarrassment.
Anyone can see the devotion she offers
is her own.

Who is she, this Belle, to be committed
to hollow plastic displays?

Things started off differently,
before her discovery
that this corporate mobile

could take off.

WHAT A FIND

Because my uncle has died
I drag to the clubhouse
a piece of warped, corrugated tin,
paint red and white stripes
for the roof.

One afternoon in New Mexico,
his spirit tells me
he is getting
a little tired,
always being on duty.

Jim lived and died
guarding someone,
somewhere.

He is a Marine,
in worlds of smashed words.

BELLE'S RAGGED ARMY

Uniforms courtesy of Mrs. Zenon Bobinski and
the Barter-Mart.

A brass bell jangles whenever customers arrive,
the Brooklyn accent calls out, "May I help you?"

This ragged army finds uniforms of dreamy ideas

> The Unicyclist spins yarn on her wheel,
> clutching a jeweled mirror.

> The Dissociative Math Whiz
> skates a private rink.

> The Bossy Mountain Man.

> The Lost Inventor.

They proceed on as Lewis and Clark of yore.
Behind every footfall,
they shake up puffs of dust,
freeing the sweetness of old ghosts.

They picnic at the
headwaters of the Missouri State Park, competing
alongside graves of diphtheria victims.

In honor of these unfortunate souls,
the children kick up old mouse bones,
skeletons of nascent dreams.

At home, Belle zips up her leopard-skin robe,
fumbles with her long black holder,
and flicks off the hot ashes.
With a moistened eye,
she utters

"My robe… it's melting."

Khufu's Boat

Montana rivers tattoo
Joseph Skyward's guitar arm.

The ink on his fingers spells out

F O O D   R E N T

I wake to a feeling
Joe has passed.

Rivers ago,
we share many rooms
in an old hotel
of double-digit rent,
bathrooms down the hall.

Holding open jagged,
can-opener spaces
for edge-people.

Knowing
his cancer means the end soon,
he records shared moments with friends,
sends them to a big cloud,
until needed.

Khufu, the Egyptian pharaoh,
builds for his father
a staggering phenomenon.
Solely with wooden planks and reed ropes,
he weaves a beautiful,
watertight boat.

Khufu buries the boat
near his river,
for forty-five hundred years,
until needed.

My Grandmother's Hands

He never covers the big hole on his neck,
sips Hamm's beer, bids cards
by knocking knuckles on the kitchen table.

In my mind's eye, Howard smells of fresh sweat,
smokes a pipe,
laughs loud,
and wears a white tank top.

Nellie meets us at the picket gate.
She opens it with patient eagerness,
touching her worn hands to our young faces,
then to her old cheeks.

Their little band heads out,
Howard drives Nellie and Brenda
through South Dakota in their new used car.

They return with full bags:

> a Hamm's Beer waterfall clock,
> their "living landscape" for the kitchen,

> plastic flowers for Uncle Jim's grave.

Marcy, the neighbor's monkey,
rattles her leash along the clothesline.

My mother says funerals are for the living.
Surely Belle is not paying close attention.

LEAVING THE TREASURE STATE

We wander south,
along the spine of the Rockies.

Rolling out after Chinook winds,
we stop for one last swim.

Above the water's edge,
raptors and airstreams circle.

A beak nods toward my dog,
the playful misstrike
from a blossoming reptile.

In my dream,
he remains a man.

DAD SAVES ME FROM DROWNING

Longing from the sky hits me on the head,
deep and blue.

I feel I am being watched.

Gently exploring the white contrails of a passing jet,
the exploding power of Jesus,
or the graveyard.

I am two years old.

The children whack away
at the tissue-paper burro,
the Earth spills sweet regalos onto children.

From the merciful quiet of the swimming pool,
submerged lights *speak* to me.

I sink into blue.

Dad plucks me out,
my insect legs cycle in mid-air.

My mother's limp hands bounce in front of her,
a Tyrannosaurus. Alone with her
and the rackety clothes dryer.

She snaps, "How could you do this to me?"
A tight-lipped percussion of shame.

"It's all because of you."

THE MOVE

I know my dumb doll stares into a lost,
unblinking space
somewhere.

"It will be replaced
once we get there," Belle says.
She takes my fluffy bear.

I am given a broadcloth substitute, striped and blue.
Its eyes fall off,
the felt vest dissolves,
its ears yellow.
I leave Belle's bear on my bed.

Russell Haverstock stinks up the whole neighborhood.
The bear's outstretched arms hang
from the rafters; he strips it of fur.
His bluish-grey flesh weeps.

Children follow their noses
to the Haverstocks' garage,
where the worn bear
hangs.

AUNT MATTIE I: KITCHEN TABLE

First, she married my Uncle Plato.

On a visit to town one day, there was a woman.
Pointing out Plato,
and within earshot,
the woman said,

>   "That's my man."

Plato had a tragic battle with the bottle.

Mattie made things work,
made things heal.

Her calling was seasonal;
she followed the harvests.

After she was through cooking,
she went about preserving,
serving every last bit,
feeding those in need.

We played a hand of seven-point pitch.
Her kitchen table had a covering where
Mattie shared things.
Smoothing the vinyl cloth in front of her,
she would say,

>   "That's how it was."

A plastic tail, a rhythmic wag, the fake dog
stares from Mattie's kitchen windowsill, yapping
at all front stoop movements.

Only seeds of *red* zinnias were saved for her
walkways.

A Big Wind

I wake up
to the cooling embers
of a dream I had not asked for.

From the banks of the Yellowstone River,
my dog brings a bleached
tree limb, tall as me.

It stands by my front door.
An old wooden box
holds its undulating girth,
a glittering blackbird becomes its hat.

In my dream,
distractions are gone,
time is gone,
souls are meeting once again.

An old Indian man on a mesa,
looks far off,
ten years away.
Sitting there beside him,
he speaks silently to me.

I wake up from looking,
follow the pull south.

At the old rest stop near Shiprock, New Mexico
there are many dogs.

One has a crooked ear angled like a tired party hat,
house paint brushed on her bony sides,
a scarred snout and recent pups.

I take her.

It is culling season on Native land,
and it is my birthday.

MY MOTHER'S HANDS

She has the biggest hands in the neighborhood.
They are stronger, even, than my father's.

They are tree-burl knuckles on night-crawler fingers.
She likes saying she can open anything.

Belle contorts her mouth, bears down,
then ends with
a twist.

She especially loves thinking about her strange talents
while shuffling cards.

With conniving eyes, she tells her children,
"I play to win."

Her hands match her massive teeth, tired jaw,
and weighty overbite.

She is most proud
when announcing to her public,

"I am here, on planet Earth
to make everything even."

A New School

Firemen hand out red plastic helmets
after the safety assembly.

We, the helmeted, are held together
in front of the school, hatchlings,
emergent through yellow crosswalk lines,
toward the world on the other side of the street.

In wild woods a turtle
with a red #3 painted on its back.
After a couple of days I take #3
to school in a cardboard box,
for Show and Tell.

When checking on the box the next morning,
#3 is not moving.

I console the class at my new school,
"I can find another."
They all laugh.

I buy a little turtle at the dime store,
take it home.

Soon, I find a hole through my turtle's back
exactly the size of a boy's index finger.

Strictly on instinct, and in tribute to Turtle's spirit,
my own shell begins assembling.

OSCAR MOVES TO ARCADIA VALLEY

There is a delicate snake that has jaunty stripes
along its spine.

Oscar catches it by the road, grabs it by its tail,
and whips it around his head—
a country boy's tilt-a-whirl.

He stops abruptly and slaps the snake
against a fence-post,
watching its head fly off.

He skins this delicate snake to make a hatband.

Oscar sees the girl from the movie screenings,
doffs his hat, then an awkward silence.

He asks the girl her name, then says,
"We had a *horse* named Belle once."

Belle asks Oscar, "What's that smell?
Is that coming from your hat?"

He explains the snake's story to her
with his very last

independent thought.

AUNT MATTIE II: BUMBLE BEES

In a buzz
they nest in the side of a dry gulch,
making their honey.

Their magics meet,
twist,
then twine.

At work all day,
for the long, hungry lines.

She holds up a ladle,
strong,
like a Marine.

She can do anything.

Mattie's apron
covers worn legs.

Her knees will not last as long as these tables.

BURNING LADY

Vladimir Putin
said today:
"Every stage in life leaves a trace."

The Burning Lady, fifty feet tall.
Crowds gather to see her, excited for
her disturbing tales,
red ashes flash into space.

She has a hunger for spirit
and eyes watching her.

Little children,
lips humming,
together at her feet.

Down, she goes down,
into the dark side,
where her sort of sadness
was once a Deadly Sin.

Astronauts claim to smell outer space.
Something burnt,
something sweet,
something,

like good intentions.

My arms twist and cross over my chest all night,
elbows throb and quiver all day,
both eyes lock.

I stare into my past.

MARSHALL KOVITZ PASSES ON

A housefly stirs me
as I learn of his death.

Bicycling in metal flocks,
uniquely devoted to balance,
even after that car broke his hip.

He never ages.
A frequency holder,
an atomic vibration clock,
not put off by naked solitude.

His true comrade is exceptional purity,
and a frayed co-op badge.

Stakes out territory on a Nob Hill of the seventies;
drives all night to get us to Montana.
Says he enjoys road trips.

"Just one thing,
I dine at roadside buffets,
like Golden Corral."

Birch Lane, Davis, CA 1962

My kitten goes to the bathroom on Belle's bed, and so,
the house falls apart.
Dad leaves with his gun.

I have a haunting dream.
I see a carnival, with all its houses:
Fun, Crazy, Fright, Mirrors.
A woman whispers, "Wonderland, Wonderland,
Wonderland."

The inconsistencies, the ignored,
the story.

She spins around.

"Who do you like better," she says,
"your mommy or your daddy?"

"Daddy."

I stand in front of him.
Tall, shimmering pheasant feathers are Scotch-taped
to my paper headband,
opalescence across my crown.

"Dad, did you shoot my Alvin cat?"
He looks straight into my eyes.

"I did."

BELLE GOES TO SAFEWAY

The Safeway grocery is at 8th and Main.
Because of the potholes, my brother Steve
calls 8th Street
the Wilderness Road.

"No one ever wants to go with me to the grocery.
It's so lonely there," she says.

Turning the wheel of her Dodge battleship,
Belle sweeps into her Safeway parking space.

She travels the aisles, directs my task.
As her personal assistant, I push her cart,
point, and retrieve everything on her list.

Listen to stories about Shur Fine canned goods,
Joyette ice cream, the Depression;
the twists of her grocery-store logic.

Belle then spots Fern, her unobtrusive clerk.

Like a cow in its final chute, the cart goes into the slip
of her Express checkout lane.
Silver-pinged squeaks circle on until the wheels meet
Fern, the most precise checker,

at Belle's Safeway.

VICTORIA

A baby laughing.
Mewing sounds,
roaring,
for the Greatest Show on Earth.

This morning,
covering her shock of black hair,
a knitted pink skull-cap,
rounding out her "animal ears,"
a vase of cut flowers graces
the table
here, in my vast palace.

The show appears and disappears,
like a world.

In magic we go to sleep,
each night,
replenishing ourselves.

All in one big sky, I tell you.

Circus excitement comes through
the veiled hint
that it could all come tumbling down.

She smiles, laughs.
Delighted, I touch her stockinged toes,
saying to her,
"Good luck."
She, with her smile, says,
"Same to you."

There are no do-overs,
that's the thrill of the circus.

She does not know this yet.

MY FEET

Victims of a toy metal drum.
The bloody easing of embarrassment.
Now, someone else will *see*
the hardship of Belle.

Sonia's hands wring the cloth,
she compresses my foot,
the screaming stops.

In front of the TV,
I put little tools under my foot callouses,
bend and snap the pins,
peel off skin from thick parts of the soft,
freshly mined quarry.

My dad would cuss when he gouged his foot
on sewing needles hiding
in our family-room carpet.

Years later, he asks Belle, and squirms,
"Which of the kids peeled the skin off their feet?"

With a smile,
and blighted eyes,
Belle points to me,

"That one."

Thomas

Handmade capes secured around his neck:
one for the laundry,
one for his drawer,
one to wear.

Older, he casts aside the little capes,
builds flimsy knee-length boots,
glues them onto soles of thin rubber.

Imagined destinations.
Old treasure maps decoded.
Blaring tin megaphones on top of rigs,
driving all night long.

Adolescents all,
speaking with unearned authority,
playing their games,
these children of Belle.

FORESTS OF MEMORY

Diagonals cut deep into the blue spruce forest
flanking our house across from Cooper Park.
Tree cutouts decorate our green shutters.

In springtime the noisy magpies build their nests
outside of her second-story window.

Belle recognizes in her many skewed mirrors a sexy,
spiritual dynamo.
She sees herself and reaches out to touch her coif.

The magpies recognize themselves
as magpies.

My father hollers over the morning racket:
"Birds, wake up. Your chicks are HUNGRY!"

So it goes, here in my house,
in the wild forests of memory.

In the end, my father says,
"Must we talk about details of the past?
What's so wrong
with
right now?"

THAT BOY

He had just gotten his driver's license.

The neighbors gather around.
She does not come to the door.

It is my father who rides with me in the ambulance
after I land on my head in the street.

Belle recalls *her* tragedy.

TORTOISE

The pioneer swims the dark current,
drags land up under her belly.

She prefers her right arm,
follows its accidental arc,
hits her nose on a stone,
slides down,
slowly starts up again,
for another go.

Strong,
under a heavenly crafted shell,
her dented geodesic dome, lovely swagger,
looks for the ancient burrow.

She will live a hundred years.

Sisyphus,
meandering endlessly,
no decreasing sense of purpose.

WILLIAM LAND PARK, SACRAMENTO,
DECEMBER, 1972

Little metal ponies,
scratched-out eyes.

Bodies welded
to rusted metal springs.

Someone's idea of the
Old Woman Who Lived in a Shoe.

My brother hitched a thousand miles.

Belle takes us to the *trying hard* park.
Crowned with paper party hats,
she thinks it will be fun for us to get some ice cream;
"DAQEER-EE ice, or WHATever you want to call it."

The ducks are calm,
paddling in circles
through grey water.

One adjusts
a coquettish wing.

BELLE HITS A DOG

She looks in the rear-view mirror,
into this dusk, looking
for old illusions.

Resentments over June's afternoon raindrops.
The scent rare, she squashes her cigarette and sniffs.
Watches the expanse of windshield
slapped by Polaris wipers.

Her low-slung machine hugs the road.
My mother is given to sailing,
handling a barge.

The barking is barely heard over the rain.
I feel its bizarre bump.

She winds her mouth to one side,

"I had no choice,
probably done this all its life."

She told me about a driver who hit
a cardboard box,

"It had a small child inside."

PARK BENCH, AUGUST A.M.,
MARY FOX PARK, ALBUQUERQUE

Her conversations
have a pickpocket's touch.

They tore down the old mansion
for this little park.

People get married here,
bring their kids to play.
It is quiet at dawn, except for the birds.

Along the curved walkway
she sits primly under a mimosa tree

says her name is Pat
but seems more like a Patricia.

I wait too long and then,
"I'm Joan."

I'm in my yard one morning.
She walks by and asks why I don't wear gloves.

I look down at my hands,
red and swollen,
caked in mud.

She compliments my blouse.

"My house is on the southeast corner over there.
My son says he needs to sell it now.
I am going to live in a rest home."

"Would it be alright if I visit this park sometimes?"

Pat's memory steals me back.

THE CATERPILLAR

I found a fuzzy-wuzzy,
the must-pet worm of our sidewalk.

Steve, aka "Tease," throws it across me,
onto Birch Lane.

"A monarch," he says.
Steve is my translator, teaching me to talk.

Into the street, I go
to get my caterpillar back.

A motorcycle comes buzzing from behind me.
For a moment, I can fly.

THIRST

I go to chisel out fossils planted in boulders,
perfect discs to make my ghostly necklace.

I ride Steve's red Schwinn down to the dirt road,
stand up on the pedals to feel tall,
throw my head back to feel free.

I start by testing, wiggle my right ankle,
rock one hinged calf, then the other,
pound my head on my pillow.

I hum my special song louder and louder,
"Da-ad, Da-ad, Da-ad.
Could you...bring me a glass of water?"

The mascots wear the hard, glazed eyes of a zoo.
I line them up on either side of my head to guard me.

My Dream of Belle

The Polaris is the widest car ever made,
designed with a stunned look on its face.
I am strapped into the vinyl world of Dodge.

From her self-proclaimed "Death Seat,"
Belle has control of our climate.

As is her habit, Belle points all vent flaps up
toward her face,
leaning low in front of the maximum AC.

The Mission Control vents point toward the ceiling.

"This gives those in the back cool air," she declares.
"It may not feel like it, but that's the way it works."

I sense her energy as she turns around to look at me.
Leaning forward on my bench seat,
my palm raises to almost touch her lips.

I spread my fingers wide so I cannot read her resolve.
Gently, I push back against her face and say,

"I'm going to tell."

THE NYLON COUCH OF OUR FAMILY ROOM

Overstuffed and covered in sculptured flora.
If we whisper we can share what we are seeing:
a word or two,
funny farm, asylum, insane.

Steve says in some places you cannot kill yourself
because it is illegal.
"It's the law," he says, "in some places."
He likes playing the older-brother card.

Dad tends the garden, soaks clematis roots,
flooding his handmade water wells.
He helps them climb their trellis stage.

Smudging for aphids with a white cloud of puff.
He trains caragana to be an archway,
marking our concrete trail to the trash.

The low running, casual hissing, tiny falling sound
of the evening water routine
means he is content.

Upstairs, I can barely hear the spigot's water flowing.
I go to sleep.

Now I wish the same for my father,
the old Ag Man.

THREADS OF LIFE

The threads of life are wallpaper.
Everywhere, but no one sees them.

Shame
whacks
my back.

For her fifty-first wedding anniversary,
Belle wears a
floor-length,
ivory,
purely acetate,
zippered affair.

Hornets' rear-ends
leave sticky nets
all around my head.
With horns on their faces,
their righteous swords
test the room's tension.

STEVE BURT 10/2/54–4/5/73

He wants interesting stands of grass for his first place.

One late-August afternoon,
Steve drives the rusty Wagoneer,
we gather wild turf
all over Gallatin Valley.

He lives between the worlds
of kitchen-table Canasta
and another.

A place without nouns.

He masters the art of spelunking,
takes his Montana State tennis team
to Davis, California.

The procession of moths in tennis whites
stays briefly in our home.
In two months he will be back at college.

He rides his golden bicycle up into Hyalite Canyon,
just before the last snowfall,
and with a blast,

he stops his own heart.

BELLE WORKS OUT

Belle goes to the basement for solitude.
She turns up Sousa's recorded marches,
gets on the stationary bike,
tilts her chin like old royalty.

She clenches her mouth.
Chews on one side of her tongue,
the part she knows will feel good,
coaxing it to be tingly and alive.
She is packing her saxophone,
leading the marching band.

Belle, before she married,
before redecorating the houses,
before she learns to entertain,
throw her head back,
laugh uproariously,
while Oscar serves drinks,
and jokes, about the mysterious
blood on the floor.

Everyone finds it funny.
Can't tell whose blood it is.

CONVERSATION WITH OSCAR

He swipes his memory,
shaving the dried edges off the past.

Gently soaking his bruised efforts
with salves of thick sweet-grass
from a green Watkins tin.

My animals are melting away.
I am singing songs,
bouncing my body,

calling after the stuffed creatures.
When we moved north
Belle, in secret, drove the herd away from me.

Oscar and I ditch the worn-out route of dementia.
For a moment he remembers
how I liked sleeping with those animals on my bed.

Spotlight Flash

Evenings of darkness, Popsicles, lightning bugs,
games of limelighted shouts.

Older brothers flashing allowances,
lights brighter than my own.

Belle sneaks up behind me.
No one around, she says,
"You are strange.
No one will ever marry you.
If they do, they will be very sad
because they will have to divorce you.
It will be all your fault."

During a fight with my father,
she tosses her wedding band
onto the lawn.

She asks me, "What is the meaning of this?"
Pressing me for a response,
my six-year-old self lies there on the lawn.
I do not speak.

"How can this be,
no beginning
and no end?"

There is an answer to her koan.
It has to do with how grass grows,
and spreads.

GRANDMA CLARCIE

Near Billings,
Clarcie laughs out loud,
visits with her bus-mate,
describes pinning money to her girdle.

In her Broken Bow kitchen, the *Secret Sister* display.
She knows where each gift came from
and when received.

Hoping I would quit biting my nails,
she sends me a manicure case with butterflies on it.
It zips. Admired, but I bite my fingernails anyway.

She orders us her neighbor's pastel lampshades,
Styrofoam egg cartons from the Hinky Dinky,
glass marbles punched into each divider.

In Heaven, we will wear clothes from Grandma.
For me, calico robes of green flowers;
flannel, leopard-skin pajamas for Sandy;
for Tom, a paisley corduroy vest.

Making something
from nothing.

THE RELAY

Hometown snapshots
from an early spring day in middle school.

In the front window of
Buttrey's Grocery,
the sun-dried old cowboy
leaned beside a synthetic horse.
A freed dancer
in an open music box.

Carmella Bobinski and her delicate partner;
so shy, I never knew her name.
My camera caught her quiet face in dappled light.
For years, I shopped those rooms
in innocent reverence.

Roy got us our first streetlight.
He was once Bozeman's police chief.
He and his wife, Lucy, played pinochle,
shuffled oversized cards,
sat in their front-room,
at a table for the legally blind.

In the lobby of the Range Hotel,
there were red-vinyl easy chairs,
welcoming warriors
homing nightly.
Practiced raconteurs,
few words about old wars.

At the check-in desk, a reserved man,
with small eyeglasses
reflecting the afternoon light.

The handing off of life,
making dreams,
solving problems,

that is art.

BELLE PASSES AWAY

This plaster baby is wonderfully bound,
struggling, a golden tiara on her head.

Belle thinks it lends an innocent look,
so we don't tell her where it came from.

She could go on forever like this,
collecting plaster babies for her front porch.

She hurls herself around,
looks for something to scratch off her final layer.

Petrified stone eunuchs
give her old spine one last scrape.

Belle squirms, sheds her skin,
passes on.

ACKNOWLEDGMENTS

I want to thank my publisher and editor Susan Gardner for her sensitive yet scalpel-wielding comments; Holly Velazquez-Duffy, my friend and comrade, for her incisive input and questions, born of experience. Gratitude to Franziska Ortega-Moore for her fierceness and assistance.

And, of course, to "The Senator" for submitting my poems without my knowledge. Finally, I have been blessed with the companionship of dogs, a vast source of poetic inspiration.

Joan Burt
Santa Fe, NM
May, 2018